The Singing Beetle

Written by Linda Strachan
Illustrated by Oliver Hurst

Collins

Poppy the beetle liked to sing.
She sang all day.
She sang if she was happy.
She sang if she was sad.

Squeak!
Squeal!
Screech!

The rest of the beetles didn't like
Poppy's singing.
They said her singing was squeaky.
No one wanted to play with Poppy.

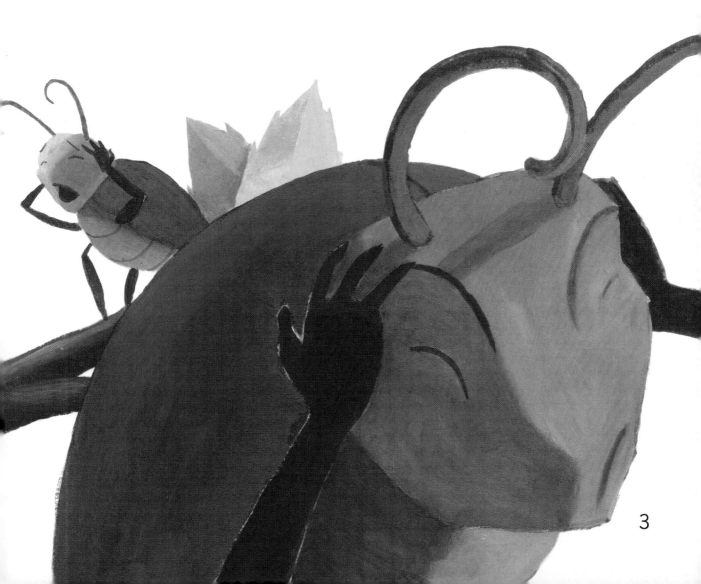

3

Poppy was sad. She went off into
the woods.
"Now I can sing as loudly as I want!"
she said.
She sang so loudly that ...

4

… she didn't spot Harry, the mouse!
Harry was looking for a treat.

Jake, the snake, was looking for
a treat, too.
"Yummy, a mouse!" he said.

But Poppy's singing was so loud ...
that Harry didn't spot Jake.

Jake looked at Harry.
Harry looked at Poppy.
Poppy looked at Jake.
"Look out, little mouse!" Poppy cried.
"A sneaky snake wants you as a snack."

Harry got a fright.
"A snake!" he said.
He ran to hide in a heap of leaves.
He tried not to shake.

Jake's tummy gave a rumble.
He went to look for Harry.
"Look out!" said brave little Poppy.

Then Poppy began to sing.
It was loud and squeaky.
Jake got a fright and he slid away.

Harry came out.

"You are a brave beetle," he said.

"And I like your singing."

"Really?" said Poppy.

Harry liked to sing, too.
"We can sing together!" he said.
So Harry and Poppy sang together,
every day.

Squeak!
Squeal!
Screech!

A story map

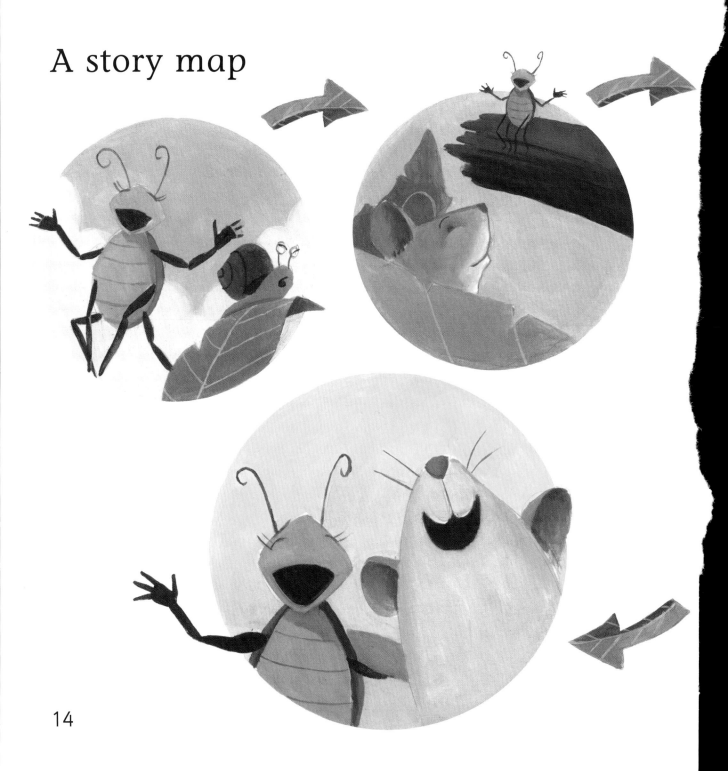

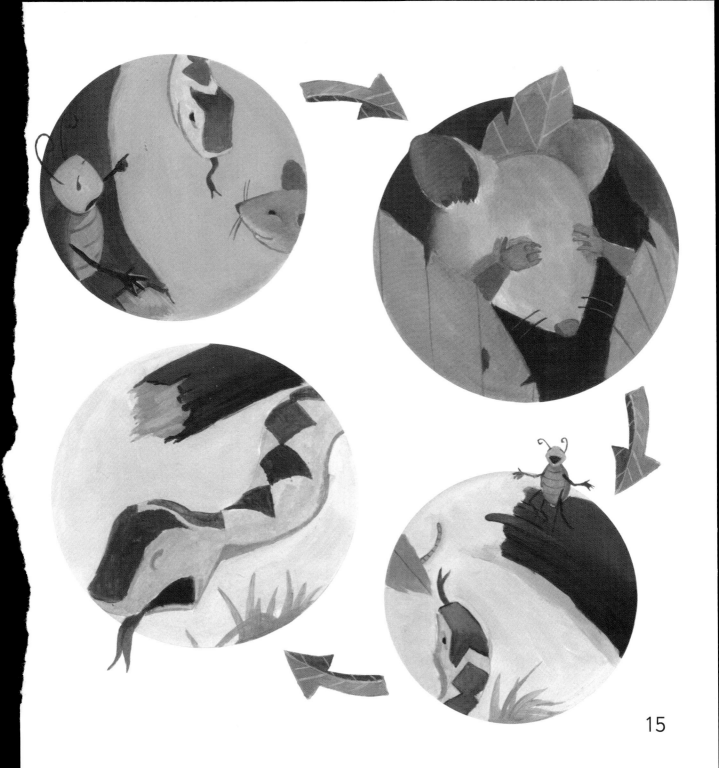

Ideas for reading

Written by Clare Dowdall, PhD
Lecturer and Primary Literacy Consultant

Learning objectives: read more challenging texts; attempt to read more complex words using phonic knowledge; recognise alternative ways of pronouncing graphemes already taught; identify the constituent parts of two and three syllable words to support the use of phonics knowledge and skills; recognise automatically an increasing number of familiar high frequency words; identify the main events and characters in stories

Curriculum links: Personal, Social and Health Education: Developing good relationships; Science: Plants and animals

Focus phonemes: ee, i-e, a-e, ea, oo, ie

Fast words: all, her, she, was, said, want(ed), I, little, want(s)

Word count: 227

Build a context for reading

- Revise the focus phonemes *ee* (beetle), *ea* (squeak), *oo* (woods), *a-e* (snake), *ie* (tried) using whiteboards. Ask children to suggest words that contain these phonemes/graphemes and model writing them.

- Read the title and back cover together. Discuss what might happen to the singing beetle in the story.

- Discuss strategies that can be used to read longer words. Model how to look for familiar word endings and to break words into constituent syllables.

Understand and apply reading strategies

- Walk through the book with the children, identifying new and fast words, e.g. squeaky, sneaky, leaves, fright.

- Ask the children to read from beginning to end, taking time to look at the pictures and use decoding skills to help read and make meaning.

- Move around the group, listening to them blending through words independently and using word knowledge to read, e.g. familiar endings.

- Invite fast finishers to reread the book with expression, using the speech and punctuation marks.